"In each person's lifetime, we will face unwanted and unwelcome change. We will also face grand opportunities. The most powerful source from which to deal with either extreme is the same. In this book, Beverly shares valuable insights on how to win—and more importantly, how to define 'winning.' This is a valuable book. I, for one, am glad she wrote it."

- Ray Edwards, Communications Strategist, Copywriter, and Author of *Writing Riches*

"Being successful often starts with how you think and is the foundation from which you build. *Win from Within* is a book that will help you establish the foundation you need to have true success."

- Os Hillman, Author of *Change Agent* and *TGIF Today God Is First*

"Beverly's book has put her on my list of favorite authors. She has allowed us to 'hear' the heartbeat of a true leader and more importantly shown us that we, too, can become a part of this symphony by following the course laid out in *Win from Within: The Heart of Success and Significance*. Bravo!"

- Susan V. Carroll, Attorney at Law

Win from Within

The Best is yet to Come!

Beverly Lewis

Win from Within:

The Heart of Success and Significance

Beverly Dru Lewis

Table of Contents

Preface

✌

"Creativity is allowing yourself to make mistakes. Art is knowing which ones to keep."
— Scott Adams

I've just returned from a long journey that took me in a giant circle and after a lot of sweat, effort and time, I ended up right back where I started.

A detour wasn't in the plan. It never is. But I learned a lot–the hard way, of course–so now I can save you some time and hopefully you can learn from my mistakes.

I've been writing for months (okay, years), knowing I have a book in me. In these past few weeks, I've come to a shocking realization. Writing hasn't flowed for me because I was writing out of my intellect rather than from my heart. And that simply won't deliver what I must give you–the heart of the matter.

My heart is in business. And business, in America, is typically treated more like science than art, when it's actually both. Science is a left-brained matter, and art functions from the right side of the brain. Business (and life), done the right way, for the right reasons, is a whole-brain function. Running a business out of the intellect, with a disconnection from the soul will be dry, mechanical, and unfulfilling.

Think of a musician who can play every note perfectly but lacks any expression or emotion in the delivery of the music. Great execution—but no heart. That's not my style. I began playing the piano before I could read and studied with a master teacher throughout my high school years. He was always rather frustrated with me because my performances lacked perfection. But because I poured my heart into the notes, making the keys weep, laugh, and dance, I consistently pulled off superior ratings in competitions.

Now I've come to realize that the key to success in business involves an element of artistry. This is central to my assignment in sharing what I've learned. It is not a formula, and no business school can teach you what I've learned the hard way. Textbooks don't contain the steps to increasing your Emotional Quotient. The answers are within you.

Have you ever known a parent who gave their children what they needed physically, but withheld love? Like the father who provides the money for food, a comfortable home and the latest in technology, but is never home. Or the mother who oversees, making sure rooms are cleaned and teeth are brushed, but withholds hugs and affection.

Think about the young people who are products of homes like that. Usually, they perpetuate the cycle by living in dysfunctional relationships. Primarily, because they don't even know what a healthy and whole home looks like.

A business is another kind of family. Far too many people don't know what a healthy one looks like. Dysfunctional workplaces result in high turnover, division, and lost productivity. Unhappy employees do not foster happy clients or customers. The pages in this book get to the heart of the matter, where success and significance are found.

Sometimes being lost is part of the journey. Going around the mountain as I wrote and doing a fair share of wandering in the dark has been a process that produced thoughts with the power to transform your business, your home, your community and your nation. It's that important.

If you are ready to exchange aggravation for anticipation, frustration for fascination, and striving for a grace-filled walk, you're in the right place. I'm glad you're here. Now we've got work to do. After 35 years of work with over 10,000 professionals, in-depth research on leadership, success, and significance, as well as lessons from my own entrepreneurial ventures, I have developed a heart full of lessons to help you on your way. It's time to cross over into the land of your rich inheritance.

Introduction

❧

"It is good to have an end to journey toward; but it is the journey that matters, in the end."
— Ernest Hemingway

It was at the end of a hike on "Perseverance Trail" northeast of Juneau, Alaska that I stumbled and fell. Crossing a creek bed over rugged terrain, I turned my ankle and went down hard. Trying to regain my footing, waves of dizziness wouldn't even allow me to stand. My husband was able to carry me on his back to the trailhead where we encountered some photographers with a vehicle nearby. (They were on the trail to photograph grizzly bears in the area–a comforting thought when you can't walk, much less run.)

Agility and sure-footedness are valuable assets when you're in the wilderness. Since I'm not particularly gifted with either of these in the physical sense, I have intentionally cultivated these assets for life and business. Perspective is a determining factor in attitude, thus I've learned that though I may fall, if I fall forward, I'm still making progress.

Even when you have to be carried, forward progress counts. But if you're the one doing the carrying, progress can be really slow with the heavy weight of someone latched onto your back. How many people can you carry like that? What if you had to carry them on your back across a raging river, leaping from stone to stone? Even the strongest among us could possibly carry just one. I couldn't even do that.

Since sure footing is invaluable, imagine that this river can be strategically crossed by stepping on a series of large stones. In addition, there is a safety line stretched from shore to shore that you can hold onto to aid in stability and balance. You still might not be capable of carrying someone across, but how many could you lead across? The possibilities are limitless.

Strategies Change, Principles Don't

In the chapters ahead, we will undertake crossing the river from the wilderness to a land of promise–a land of success, significance and satisfaction. A place where your gifts, talents and experience converge and your life becomes a fulfillment of your destiny.

The stepping stones are solid–I've tested and tried them. I've made the journey across successfully, and now it is my turn to show others the way. I've been on the river in seasons of powerfully rushing waters that roil and tumble with the threat of knocking you off your feet. And I've seen the creek bed dry up in drought conditions–a rugged gully of stones and debris. Through it all, the stepping stones remain, firm and unchanging. I know the way across–follow me.

Chapter 1
Overcoming Fear

ℒ

"Everything you want is on the other side of fear."
— Jack Canfield

I love living on the Gulf Coast in Florida and marvel at the natural beauty every time I travel over the numerous bridges in our area. However, just because we're called The Sunshine State doesn't mean it is always sunshine and light around here.

I recall a particularly distressing trip across a bridge one dark and stormy night. This was not just any bridge; this was the 4.1-mile long Sunshine Skyway Bridge at the mouth of Tampa Bay. Late one night, I finished a meeting and headed to Sarasota where my children were staying with my parents. This mammoth bridge stood between me and my destination. In fair weather, the soaring span offers a breathtaking view— not appreciated much by those afraid of heights. In windy weather, it's a real nail-biter. This particular night, I had the triple fear-factor of nighttime, high winds, and driving rain. Oh–did I mention I was alone?

You might ask, "What could happen? This is a roadway that is part of an Interstate Highway." Well, believe me, it was in the front of mind what not only *could* happen but *had* happened. I had watched with morbid fascination all the news accounts of a disaster that happened early one morning during a thunderstorm. A freighter struck a support column of the bridge, causing six cars, a truck, and a Greyhound bus to plummet into the water, killing 35 people. Not a great thing to be thinking about as I prepared to travel the same bridge in such a storm.

As my heart rate accelerated, I considered my options. It would take hours to go around and take another route. If I spent the night without crossing the bridge, I would have to call and wake up the household, no doubt scaring my mom to pieces. I determined I had to press through the fear and just make the trip over. I gripped the steering wheel, said a prayer, and began to sing my way across the bridge.

What bridge do you need to sing yourself across? It may be a financial obstacle, a change in career, re-defining yourself after a divorce–it could be any number of things. The statistical ranking of the top ten fears in all the world puts public speaking as the number one fear in the world. Death is number two, and the fear of spiders and other arachnids is third.

Humor is a common antidote for fear. Jerry Seinfeld quips, "According to most studies, people's number one fear is public speaking. Number two is death. Death is number two. Does that sound right? This means to the average person, if you go to a funeral, you're better off in the casket than doing the eulogy." It only wastes time and energy to be afraid of death. If you are going to be afraid, better to fear a life unlived.

The good news is that fear is a perfectly normal emotion, and we all feel it. If you are not experiencing it, you aren't doing enough new things. Fear is like fire, it can heat a house and cook your dinner or it can burn you down. It's not about eliminating the fear. It's learning to take the small steps that move you through it. Walking forward through the fear can take you to a new place of fresh courage and strength. In that place, you have the joy of victory and are in a position to now help someone else become a victor in that area.

Eleanor Roosevelt advised, "Do one thing every day that scares you." Have you noticed how often fear is accompanied by fascination? We want to observe the rattlesnake or the sharks from behind the glass, and dream of doing daring things like jumping out of airplanes. The challenge is to use the sharp edge of fear to do something useful.

Identify the fascinating fear that is connected with your gifts and talents–your calling. What is it that you long to do–BUT. Yes, the thing that has the big BUT in the way. Follow these 4 steps to begin the journey from fear to faith.

1) Make a plan. You don't have to face the fear yet, you just have to plan to face the fear. Don't fret about it. Allow your pride and fascination with making a plan to dominate your thoughts.

2) Take the first step. Action in increments–inch by inch, it's a cinch.

3) Keep taking steps until there is no turning back. This should involve a verbal declaration of your goal–even if that is to only one accountability partner. Remember when you were a kid and you climbed all the way to the high dive? Once you are up there, it's harder to climb down the steps backwards than to jump–especially if the steps are lined with other kids waiting impatiently for their turn.

4) Celebrate each step. Don't wait until you reach an epic milestone to celebrate. Take pleasure in the progress

and congratulate yourself as you go.

If you want something you've never had, you'll have to do something you've never done. You have to leave the land of your comfort to cross the bridge to your destiny. Don't look back, hold back or hesitate. Feel the fear and do it anyway. You are not alone.

If you knew you couldn't fail, what would you do next?

Chapter 2
Core Values

ℒ

"It's not hard to make decisions once you know what your values are."
— Roy Disney

I still have a set of keys my grandfather gave me decades ago. The worn leather strap holds keys of many shapes, sizes and colors–ranging from antique to dated to modern. The timeworn skeleton key is most distinctive and opened a door to a happy place filled with a lifetime of memories. My 98-year-old grandmother had no interest in updating the lock on her front door, even though its use required familiarity and knowing how to jiggle the key just so to gain access. Forget it if you were in a hurry–that lock required patience and experience to operate, or you could spend the better part of an hour jabbing a piece of metal into a hole with absolutely no results. But the keeper of the key knew the secret of how to lift and apply exactly the right pressure to hear the gratifying click of the open mechanism.

A set of keys provides an interesting profile of what we have permission to access. The people we do life with have duplicates of some of the same keys we have, but most key rings are unique.

The core values we carry in life are like a set of keys–they indicate the doors we will open. Your personal keys are critical for accessing those things that are uniquely important to you. What we value, we have access to. Interestingly, often values are accessed only on a visceral level. If you fail to be consciously aware of your core values, you will miss the opportunity to intentionally align yourself with the people and assignments that fit your mission and purpose. Small keys can unlock big doors and deeply-rooted values are linchpins to our future.

Values are central principles serving as an end in themselves, rather than a means to an end. Without them, accomplishments would be shallow and meaningless. Our values cause us to make decisions intuitively. They are often the unconscious, unseen, and unacknowledged settings that serve as the steering committee for our choices. Most of the decisions we make every day are small ones and are based on habitual responses. Sometimes, the small choices are based on our desire to please ourselves or others. Little things become big things, and that's why staying connected with core values in all we do is a big deal.

The impact of our values on our lives is massive. Core values are like the submerged portion of an iceberg. Our behavior equates to the visible portion of an iceberg, which typically represents a mere 10% of the mass and substance. Ninety percent of what makes you tick is in the subconscious realm.

Core values are shaped in our early years, largely by what is modeled by parents, teachers, and mentors. Thankfully for those who didn't have the fortune of positive role models, values can change. Lives are transformed when there's a shift in core values.

I've seen it happen when a friend got cancer and recovered to appreciate a second chance to live fully. I've witnessed it when someone close experienced a spiritual awakening. I've watched another hit rock bottom—losing family, job, finances, and freedom, to then experience the deep shift that equipped them to rebuild on a new, solid foundation.

I've seen a major shift in values come with parenthood—the ultimate leadership challenge. The weight of the responsibility for the well-being and development of an innocent little person can be a wake-up call to get anchored to core values.

Any wake-up call that demands a focus on what is truly important in life can be a good thing. However, I prefer to live with eyes wide open and heart tuned to the symphony of all that is good rather than wait for a cataclysmic event to hurtle me into awareness.

The unique combination of values that forms your personal identity is the master code for your life. You can change the combination when you connect your head and your heart and make sure all the parts align.

When I work with leaders on core values, I notice it's easy to give mental assent to a long list of values. So how do you refine the list and find the pure gold of the central values that govern your life?

First, think of three people you admire and respect—people who have had a major influence in your life. Sometimes, celebrity and historical figures make the list. Often, mothers, fathers, and grandparents are in this roll call. Next, write down several characteristics of each of these people. What do you love about them? Now, look at the characteristics they share. This exercise will direct you to the three to five values that are central to who you are.

Living out of these principles is a key to your success and

happiness. When you adopt behaviors that aren't rooted in these values, your life becomes incongruent, and you won't be content.

As you consider the values that are non-negotiable in your life, you can use this list of common core values to stir your thinking:

Peace
Justice
Happiness
Success
Relationships
Fame
Authenticity
Influence
Power
Faith/Hope
Wealth
Honesty
Integrity
Respect for Self
Respect for Others
Responsibility
Courtesy
Loyalty
Enjoyment
Recognition/Expertness
Family/Community
Wisdom
Status/Prestige
Location
Creativity
Health
Service
Generosity
Independence

Invest the time to become conscious of the values that are key to your well-being. Then go to the next level. When you care enough to discover the keys carried by your family, friends, and co-workers, the doors that open before you will astonish and delight you.

What are your five core values?

Chapter 3
Beyond Disappointment

⚴

"Footfalls echo in the memory down the passage which we did not take towards the door we never opened..."
– T. S. Eliot

When I was a kid, I loved a game show Monty Hall hosted called "Let's Make a Deal." There were opportunities to win prizes that were hidden behind three curtains or doors. If you chose the right one, you won something awesome, like a new car. The wrong door held dud prizes; a donkey, a pile of dirt–they were quite creative at coming up with devastatingly disappointing duds that made the audience roar with laughter.

How many of you have ever chosen the wrong door? Yeah, me too. We've all made some choices that didn't work out. I can give you the positive spin that there's no such thing as failure–only outcomes. And if it didn't come out the way you wanted, you can go at it again. The spin doesn't erase the internal damage that takes place. Shame, hurt, disappointment, and disillusionment can take up residence in our minds and hearts.

The aftermath of lingering regret can be far worse than the event. As a native Floridian, I've seen a good number of hurricanes. Just a few years ago, a rather minor hurricane made landfall more than a hundred miles west of us. The storm surge took out the foundation of a family beach home. It had weathered much bigger storms, but the house was a total loss from this small storm because the waves undermined the very foundation. That's exactly what disappointment can do in our lives.

In a study by Mike Morrison of the University of Illinois and Neal J. Roese of Northwestern, 370 Americans were interviewed about their life's deepest regrets. Lost loves and unfulfilling relationships turned out to be the most common regrets, though women had far more romantic regrets than men. Family matters were the second greatest source of regret. Interestingly, people regretted inaction far longer than actions.

Another interesting study reports the insights of a nurse, Bronnie Ware, who spent decades caring for people in their last days on earth. She noticed there were five top regrets expressed by these people in their recollections:

1) I wish I'd had the courage to live a life true to myself, not the life others expected of me.
2) I wish I hadn't worked so hard.
3) I wish I'd had the courage to express my feelings.
4) I wish I had stayed in touch with my friends.
5) I wish that I had let myself be happier.

Regret management is a psychological concept that means leaving the past where it belongs–behind us. We can learn from it and ultimately have to forgive ourselves in order to move forward. Often, that's easier said than done because of the emotional tentacles that have to be unwrapped from our hearts. This is a non-elective surgery if you want to be free to move forward with hope and expectancy.

Hold fast to your sense of worthiness. A sense of worthiness comes from a strong sense of love and belonging. Your life has purpose. You are here for a reason and there's no one else that brings to the world what you do.

So let's make a deal. Determine you will begin here and leave the past where it belongs and move boldly into the future. You have yet to see the full manifestation of the life that is within you. Today's the day to trade your disappointment for...your destiny.

If you knew that 20 years from now you would regret not doing something that is on your heart to do, would you do it?

Chapter 4
Vision

"You cannot depend on your eyes when your imagination is out of focus."
— *Mark Twain*

When I was in fourth grade, I had the habit of sitting at the front of the class. I got teased for this by classmates who thought I was trying to impress the teacher with my eagerness. One day, Mrs. Allen got tired of my habit of continually turning around to talk to my neighbors (imagine that!) and moved me to the last seat in the back of the room as punishment. Over the next few weeks, my grades plummeted. Was it shame? Depression? Lethargy? No. It was a vision problem. I couldn't see the work on the board accurately, resulting in what appeared to be careless mistakes. I'll never forget my awe and wonder the day I got glasses. I had no idea that you could see the leaves in trees without actually climbing the tree. The world became vivid, clear, and much more interesting.

Have you had a vision check lately? Just as you can't drive and operate a vehicle without passing a vision test, it will be close to impossible to stay on the path to success if you can't see where you are going. Have you ever driven a car blindfolded? I didn't think so—that's a wreck just waiting to happen. Writing your vision down allows you 20/20 vision. There's something miraculous and yet scientific that takes place in the mind when we connect our hopes and aspirations with a tangible vision board.

The top three reasons for writing out your vision:

1) Without a reason *why*, any price is too high when it comes to finding the energy to press on when you don't feel like it.
2) Your happiness depends on it. One of three factors that contribute to 90% of your happiness is the positive expectation and the emotions generated by anticipating doing something you love.
3) You can't hit a target you can't see.

I regularly work with teams on creating vision boards. For years, I resisted doing the actual exercise of bringing magazines, scissors, poster board, markers, and glue in to the board room, thinking it seemed a little elementary. Scratch that—it was Einstein who said, "Creativity is intelligence having fun." It doesn't matter if you feel a little silly and childish. It's vital to loosen up, laugh, and begin to dream again.

Our vision—thus our expectations—are either based on memory or imagination.

That's why children are so good at dreaming, and young people tend to be full of zeal and optimism. For them, the pull of the future is stronger than the entanglements of the past. Then we grow up. Memories have deep roots that can choke out our hopes and dreams.

If you limit your choices for the future to what seems realistic or practical, you disconnect from what you truly want, and all that is left is compromise. What began as a quest for your destiny can become a half-hearted attempt to camp in a place you were never meant to stay—you settle. You start to see the enormity of the obstacles instead of the thrill of possibilities.

In order to break through the habit of limited thinking, you have to stretch your mind. In *The Dream Manager* by Matthew Kelly, he poses a challenge to list 100 dreams. As a bona fide visionary, I assumed this would be a simple exercise for me. To my surprise, I got stuck after 76. The goal is to record all of them in one sitting—allowing an hour to do so. I had to take a break and come back to it before I was able to finish.

When people participate in the vision board exercise for the first time, they often limit themselves by thinking in terms of material achievements. True happiness requires that we think bigger than that. Here are twelve areas to consider as you freshen up your goals and dreams. How long has it been since you've let your imagination run wild?

Physical **Emotional**
Intellectual **Spiritual**
Psychological **Material**
Professional **Financial**
Creative **Adventure**
Legacy **Character**

There's no doubt that the world we live in is a blistering mess. That's exactly why we need to press in for the miraculous. I've tasted the fruit from the other side of the river, and you are going to find that it is worth the effort to make the journey to cross over.

Your vision is the artistic design for the future.

If you don't know where you're going, any road will take you there. Make your vision plain so you can run with it. Taking the extra time now to optimize your vision will save unnecessary delays caused by dead ends and detours.

What is your deepest secret desire?
Where is it written, and when did you last look at it?

Chapter 5
Resolve

❧

"Obstacles can not crush me. Every obstacle yields to stern resolve. He who is fixed to a star does not change his mind."
— Leonardo da Vinci

I have never been a runner. Matter of fact, exercise has always been sheer discipline for me and not particularly enjoyable. Yet I recently ran a half-marathon. I'll tell you how that transpired. The benefits outweighed the cost, enabling me to do something I'd never imagined myself doing.

Meet Resolve—the undeniable power of a made-up mind and a force to be reckoned with. There's a lot of talk about the necessity of passion these days. It's said that if you do what you love and love what you do, there's no stopping you.

I beg to differ. The exhilaration of doing what you love is undeniable. But crucial accomplishments are often obtained when you choose to do what is good and right, whether you feel like it or not. Character is following through with a good thing, even when the mood has left you. And trust me, the mood *will* leave you at some point during the journey to your goal.

When the elements of determination, focus, a specific goal, and a decision come into alignment, it's like the tumblers in a lock falling into place to open the door to accomplishment.

Decision time—we've all danced around it. The benefits of agility, fitness, and increased strength and stamina beckoned to me as I considered the commitment to run. I carefully considered the pros and cons and discussed my thoughts with my husband. I'll confess, I was hoping he would talk me out of it with the excuses that were already in my head. *You might get hurt. How will you squeeze in all the extra hours required for training? You've never been a runner—isn't it crazy to start this late in the game?* Instead of validating my doubts, my family was wildly encouraging.

There were additional early signs that helped me move from thinking to action. Since I had never even run a 5K, I figured I'd better find out what participating in an event was all about. The first one that fit my schedule was sponsored by the local Bar Association, as in attorneys—not purveyors of alcoholic beverages. The name, Race Judicata, was a play on the Latin term *res judicata* that means a final decision has been made and is no longer subject to appeal. A fortuitous name, indeed.

While training in Florida's ninety degree heat and oppressive humidity, I needed plenty of those types of reminders to see this through. As I pushed into the ten-mile distance in training, I realized this was harder than I anticipated. But by this time, I had told all my friends (and blogged about my intention), so the accountability factor was big.

When I crossed the finish line, I was relieved and gratified. Oh, did I mention I was exhausted almost to the point of delirium? The enthusiasm of those that cheered me on was humbling.

Have I become a marathon runner as a result of this experience? No. And again, no. I still don't love running, although I do about three miles every day. There are lots of side benefits from running, but the constant reminder that I can do almost anything I set my mind to do fuels my motivation for many things (including writing the book you hold in your hands).

For decades, the world has remembered the famous speech Winston Churchill delivered to a beleaguered Great Britain during World War II: "Never, never, never give up." He also said, "It is not enough that we do our best, sometimes we must do what is required." Profoundly wise words.

So where does quitting fit into this picture? The reality is it's humanly impossible to finish every single thing we start, to keep every single promise we make, and to have happy endings to every situation in life.

I've seen people hang onto relationships that were so completely destructive that it almost destroyed their very life. We see this in domestic violence cases. I've seen people ride a business into bankruptcy when decisions could have been made to prevent the total devastation to multiple families. But those decisions involved what seemed like giving up on a dream.

There are two ways to quit: by default or by design. Quitting by default is never desirable. That's when despair distorts reality, and we lose hope. Perhaps discouragement and loss of confidence gave way to indifference and lack of motivation.

If giving up is on your radar, examine your motives. Some of the symptoms of lost motivation include (but are not limited to) lack of focus, lethargy, loss of concentration, and procrastination. You may be really busy–but not productive, unable to finish what you've started and highly critical of yourself. If your world shrank, and you are unable to see options–this is not the time to quit. My philosophy is that if you are lost in a dark tunnel, keep going until you see the light again.

Discouragement is the enemy of your destiny. When I'm discouraged, I find strength by looking at the example of others who refused to give up. I've watched and admired Diana Nyad who became the first person to swim from Cuba to Florida without the help of a shark cage in 2013 at the age of 64. She accomplished this remarkable feat on her fifth try to complete the approximately 110-mile swim. Her first attempt was in 1978, and she was unsuccessful in her repeated attempts in 2011 and 2012. As she clambered from the water after nearly 53 hours, she said, "I have three messages. One is, we should never, ever give up. Two is, you're never too old to chase your dream. Three is, it looks like a solitary sport, but it is a team." A long-time friend said, "I always thought she could do it given her internal energy, her mental and physical strength, her will of iron." Where do you find internal energy and a will of iron? Deep. Really deep. You have to dive deep to tap into the drive that got you started on your journey. Drive is often based on what a person believes about their own abilities, not on how objectively talented they actually are.

We've established you shouldn't quit by default, but quitting by design is another matter altogether. Seasons change, and old ways don't open new doors. Sometimes you have to let something die in order to have new life come forth. I've experienced seasons of pruning in my life when it was time to relinquish positions and let go of activities that I really enjoyed. In nature, pruning is designed to allow the vine to produce more abundant and sweeter fruit. The process holds true in our lives as well. Resolve can be applied to the choice to quit something by design. It's not often easy.

Resolve is the impetus that keeps us moving forward in the face of difficulties and distractions. There are very few victories of great consequence in our lives that are gained immediately.

Progress is a process. Don't give up. Don't give in. Don't ever stop trying. The world has yet to see the full manifestation of what you are capable of. We're waiting.

What remarkable accomplishment is waiting for your decision to do what's necessary?

Chapter 6
Discipline

✑

"Discipline is the bridge between goals and accomplishment."
– Jim Rohn

C ountry living has provided an education far outside the realm of anything I have previously experienced. I've been listening to our young rooster at crowing practice for a week. Poor guy. He was born to crow, designed to crow, and it's his purpose in life to crow. But if I had recorded his first few practice sessions, you would be highly entertained. He was hilarious—sounded both sick and silly at the same time. He's been at it consistently and he has improved. But his "cock a doodle doo" is still pitiful. Who knew that roosters had to practice?

What's the difference between a pianist and someone who just plays the piano? Practice. What about running? Are you a "runner" just because you can break into a sprint if something is chasing you? Or is it when you intentionally and consistently run that you're actually a "runner"?

It's easy to look at top performers in any field and admire their gifts and talents. But how much of that actually contributes to remarkable success?

Talent is overrated. So says Geoff Colvin, author of *Talent Is Overrated: What Really Separates World-Class Performers from Everybody Else*. Colvin builds a case that the proven road to success is based on deliberate practice rather than natural giftedness. It is quite interesting to study the real story behind extraordinary performers from Mozart to Tiger Woods. They have a lot in common. Most stars were coached and groomed from a very early age by parents who were focused mentors and coaches. In fact, Colvin proposes that becoming extremely good at anything is almost impossible without a teacher or coach, at least in the early going. Without a clear, unbiased view of performance, developing the appropriate practice activity is almost impossible. The challenge is to identify one or two sharply defined areas that need to be improved along with a strategy for deliberate practice. Practice without feedback is particularly ineffective.

It's really discouraging to consistently try to get better at something without seeing any measurable progress. The difference between just putting in time and deliberate practice is defined by moving out of your comfort zone and into the learning zone. Only activities that keep us in the learning zone actually contribute to growth and improvement. However natural it is to continually do what is familiar, the pull of the comfort zone can lull us into the sand trap of mediocrity. There are three learning zones: the comfort zone, the learning zone, and the panic zone. As the name implies, the panic zone is remarkably unproductive because all one's energy is spent dealing with fear and anxiety. Excellence comes by consistently living in the learning zone.

Doing things we do well is inevitably enjoyable. Thus, a qualification of effective practice is that it's not particularly enjoyable because it's hard! The willingness to consistently do an activity that is not easy or fun is the most distinguishing characteristic identifying the best from the rest. To grow, you have to go to the cutting edge of your competence and keep going. You can expect to feel insecure and probably cranky as you stretch beyond your previously prescribed boundaries.

The power of preparation, perseverance, and practice cannot be underestimated. Malcolm Gladwell writes about the 10,000 hour phenomenon in his book, *The Outlier*, as he examines the factors contributing to high levels of success. His deduction that most masters of their craft put in 10,000 hours of practice before they became extraordinary is somewhat intimidating, but certainly makes a case for discipline.

Overnight success stories seem enticing but when you dig a little deeper, there's cause for concern. Take the history of lottery winners. The National Endowment for Financial Education estimates that as many as 70% of Americans who experience a sudden windfall will lose that money within a few years. As a whole, their stories are rather sad. They didn't have to show forth any discipline to become wealthy and thus didn't have the necessary discipline to enable them to hold on to their money.

The journey to success is a cycle–a process. Process, by definition, means "a continuous action, operation, or series of changes taking place in a definite manner." It often takes sheer discipline to carry on.

Haven't mastered that new language yet? *Press on.*
Haven't achieved your career goals yet? *Press on.*
Haven't hit your target income yet? *Press on.*
Haven't experienced ideal communication in key relationships yet? *Press on.*
Haven't seen the manifestation of your dreams yet? *Press on.*

Most success requires the fortitude of an endurance runner rather than a sprinter. Life is a long-distance run.

The revelation that talent is overrated can either intimidate you or motivate you. Either way, it strips away excuses.

The most important question to ask is not
"What am I getting?"
The most important question to ask is
"What am I becoming?"

Chapter 7
Equilibrium

❧

*"Emotional self-control–delaying gratification and stifling impulsiveness–
underlies accomplishment of every sort."*
– Daniel Goleman

It was an encounter with the Dueling Dragon, an aptly named roller coaster at Universal Studios, that convinced me my days of upside-down adventures were over forever. Children love wild rides at fairs and amusement parks. But there comes an age when the spirit wants to play, but the body screams, "No, not that way!" It's a milestone of sorts when the thrill of spinning, jerking, and feeling the crazy sensations that drop your stomach to your toes then pitch it right up into your heart is replaced by trepidation.

You may call it age. I call it wisdom. There's no shame in valuing stability and equilibrium. We typically discover the boundaries of physical change the hard way when the carnival excitement is replaced by a queasy dizziness that makes the sideline wonderfully appealing.

It was an epiphany the day I realized that being led by emotions is similar to strapping yourself into a roller coaster that won't let you off. It's utterly exhausting. There's an ancient parable that describes this see-saw vividly, though the farmer in the story seems to keep a balanced perspective. So the story goes…

A farmer had only one horse. One day, his horse ran away.

His neighbors said, "I'm so sorry. This is such bad news. You must be so upset."

The man just said, "We'll see."

A few days later, his horse came back with twenty wild horses following. The man and his son corralled all twenty horses.

His neighbors said, "Congratulations! This is such good news. You must be so happy!"

The man just said, "We'll see."

One of the wild horses kicked the man's only son, breaking both his legs.

His neighbors said, "I'm so sorry. This is such bad news. You must be so upset."

The man just said, "We'll see."

The country went to war, and every able-bodied young man was drafted to fight. The war was terrible and killed every young man, but the farmer's son was spared, since his broken legs prevented him from being drafted.

His neighbors said, "Congratulations! This is such good news. You must be so happy!"

The man just said, "We'll see."

This farmer is an improbable example of someone who is steady and unflappable. As an expressive personality, I just can't relate. I've had days when I've had enough ups and downs before lunch to wear anyone out. Good news or a successful outcome, and I'd be soaring like a bird. A disruptive phone call, a cancellation, or some other disappointment, and I'd be knocked to the ground. I'm tempted to congratulate you if you have no idea what it feels like to live at the end of a bungee cord. But empathy is called for. Look around you. I'm certain there are people in your life who experience this.

Before we go any further, I have to defend the value of emotions. Logic doesn't provoke us to action—emotion does. Emotion energizes and inspires creativity. Putting the intellect in the driver's seat has just as many pitfalls as being steered by emotion. Paralysis by analysis is just one of the traps for those governed by logic. What we really need is to find that sweet spot that allows just the right balance of the two.

One way to find balance is by teaming with people with different strengths. The dynamics of logic and emotion are often harnessed in impressive ways when opposite personality types are able to work together in harmony. Inevitably, there's tension in such a team, but with eyes on the goal and a focus on creating something that is bigger than yourself, the synergy can yield powerful results.

The blend of women and men in the marketplace are another example of the way we are designed to balance one another. Sometimes, women are maligned for being too emotional in a business setting. No doubt, there are scores of differences in the way men and women express emotion and feelings. Women are more likely to cry when extremely frustrated or embarrassed. Men are more likely to react in anger—the socially acceptable form of emotional expression for males. We are overdue in acknowledging that feelings have weight and are as appropriate in the board room as the living room.

What an arid environment we would live and work in if we tried to squeeze the emotion out of our interactions. It might be tempting to think there would be less drama, but executing tasks mechanically is the goal only if you're talking about machines or computers. People are inevitably emotional beings. It's fundamentally unhealthy to divorce ourselves from our hearts and deep emotions. Consider a doctor who stays emotionally distant from his patients in an effort to maintain clinical perspective and guard from caring too much about the individual. The resulting bedside manner is usually perceived as detached and uncaring. Is that the kind of health professional you want on your team when making critically important decisions? I think not.

Dr. William Magee states, "Reason leads to conclusion. Emotion leads to action."

The magical place of equilibrium is found intentionally. The key to keeping the heart fully engaged while resisting impulsive decisions based on the moment's emotions is in self-awareness. This awareness includes your mind, will, emotions, and physical well-being.

1) Respond rather than react. Whoever came up with the idea of counting to three (or ten, depending on the intensity of the emotion) should have patented the concept. It really helps. Take a deep breath. Pause.

2) Limit sugar and watch your diet. Seriously. Sugar, nicotine, caffeine, and other addictive substances create wild blood sugar swings and influence your mood.

3) Take B-Complex vitamins. This may seem very simplistic, but B-Complex vitamins are not stored in your body and are depleted by stress along with a long list of other culprits that can leave you deficient. The most common deficiency symptoms of B-Complex are irritability, fatigue, and mood swings. I rest my case.

4) Take a step back and ask the question, "A year from now, how important will this issue be?" "What about five years from now?" These questions will help restore your perspective about the urgency and weight of the circumstance you are dealing with.

5) Take a walk. Preferably outside. Dr. James Levine, in

a study published in *Mayo Clinic Proceedings*, reminds us that the health benefits of walking include a measurable improvement in blood pressure, joint problems, metabolic and cardiovascular disorders as well as mental health. This is not news to most of us, but the distance between knowledge and application can be huge.

These tips are some of my "go-to" stress management techniques, since being led by emotions is certainly a study in stress management.

Life is a process of transformation and there are tons of ups and downs. Excellence is a process of learning how to ride day in and day out on a somewhat even keel. I knew an athletic coach who called it "standard of performance." The players he counted on to win were not necessarily the most talented. But they were the ones who showed up for practice every day whether they felt like it or not and played well consistently.

I determined years ago to be that kind of player–the one you can count on to show up and be steady. There is no such thing as great talent without great willpower. Willpower isn't something that gets handed out to some and not to others. It is a skill you can develop. You can choose to be led by your core values rather than your emotions.

I've traded the roller coaster for a steadier ride on a track of my own design. I don't miss the drama.

What (or who) pushes the drama button in your life? What one tip will you implement to stop the ride?

Chapter 8
Authenticity

᪄

"Everything will line up perfectly when knowing and living the truth
becomes more important than looking good."
– Alan Cohen

Deception is deadly to relationships, whether it's in business or private life. When our son was five years old, his imagination did a number on our family dynamics. He began to tell his teachers and friends about his mean stepmother. Mind you, I am not his stepmother, nor did one exist in reality. But I could always tell when he'd had opportunity to talk freely to adults, as they would begin to regard me with suspicion and distrust. But he didn't really make her up; he simply was growing into the ability to separate reality from fantasy. I didn't take it personally and we still laugh about it.

An adult's inability to separate the truth from a lie isn't a laughing matter. Some adults are still living in the shadow land that young children pass through. It isn't that they think King Kong will come stomping through their neighborhood–it's a much bigger danger. When you have listened to a lie repeatedly, especially when the lie comes from your own lips, that belief becomes your reality.

This came up recently while talking to a business owner about his disappointment in people–so many don't keep their word or pay their bills–and it's people you would least expect that behavior from. Most of those people probably think of themselves as trustworthy, upstanding citizens. Since they lie to themselves (better known as excuses and justification), they are blinded to the fact that they are letting everyone else down. They are literally living in the shadow land of their own distorted perceptions.

These are the people that grin and shake your hand heartily in public but have a past due balance of $1,000, which would pay some pressing bills on your desk. It's the woman loudly criticizing over-spending in a budget meeting who is up to her neck in credit card debt from an over-indulgent lifestyle. It's the man committed to exposing political corruption who gets arrested for exposing himself to children.

Disappointing. Sometimes, devastatingly so. You thought you knew someone and find out they are not the person they appeared to be. It's especially awful to wake up to discover that you've been duped by the person you married and have been living with a person who has a secret life. It's disgusting when you can't find the truth amidst the lies. (Thankfully, I don't have personal knowledge of this but have stood beside a friend going through a hellish divorce who did.) How do you protect yourself from people like that?

First, look inside your own life. Are you walking in the integrity you expect from others? It's easy to chuckle at a child's inability to know that Mickey Mouse isn't real, but what about the destructive belief systems you've lived with so long they've taken on a life of their own?

Second, be discerning. Look beneath the surface and listen to more than words. We don't have to be distrustful, but we do have to be wise. I want to surround myself with people whose actions are congruent with their talk. Jim Rohn taught success principles to thousands, and one of his admonitions was, "You become like the five people you spend the most time with." Even when it comes to customers and clients, think twice before doing business with people of questionable character. You don't need the money as much as you might think. Peace of mind is far more valuable than padding your bank account.

Surround yourself with people of integrity. Training in identifying counterfeit currency begins with studying genuine money. Just as there are certain identifying characteristics in authentic money, so it goes with people. I grew up hearing, "you're known by the company you keep" and "birds of a feather flock together." Like so much advice dispensed by my mother, I wanted to dismiss it. However, it turns out she was right. A wise proverb says, "A mirror reflects a man's face, but what he is really like is shown by the kind of friends he chooses." Learn what is true and honorable by intentionally filling your life with people who not only believe it, but live it.

Develop a team of trusted advisors. This should be people who know you well and won't hesitate to speak the truth in love to you, whether it's about your own decisions or your attitude about the actions of others. Invite their input. One simple question can lead to major revelations: "How am I doing with…?" Ask. Sometimes that's all that's needed to get feedback that will save you from some major mistakes.

Lastly, do a regular reality check. Are you being true to your own core values? Do you need to clean up some issues you've gotten sloppy in? It's easier to make course corrections when you are only slightly off-kilter than if you ignore the creep of bad habits until you have a big problem.

Keep it real. You're walking in integrity when the life you are living on the outside matches who you are inside.

What are you allowing in your life that is not part of your ideals?

Chapter 9
Rejection

&

"Experience: that most brutal of teachers. But you learn, my God do you learn."
— C. S. Lewis

As I listened to the ringing tones click over to voice mail for the umpteenth time, my face flushed with embarrassment. No one else was looking, but I still felt red-faced and rejected as I pictured Ethan looking at the caller ID and refusing to speak to me. I disconnected the call rather than leave yet another voice message that would be ignored. Apparently, our relationship was over.

This was not some random relationship causing me to feel the acute let-down that accompanies being dumped. This was a business mentorship I had invested in—an advisor I had come to trust. Who incidentally had been paid up front for many hours of consulting I had not received.

No one likes to be snubbed. From dating blues to career shoes, it hurts when others cut you off—especially when you don't see it coming. You can try to convince yourself, "It's not personal—this is business." Good luck with that. Business is personal and rejection stinks in any setting.

As I thought through what to do about the mentor that disappeared, I searched for the lessons and what I was supposed to learn from the situation. Unfortunately, I realized I had treated people in a very similar manner during a career change years before. I sold a business and determined that in order for the new owner to establish their leadership with the team of salespeople that were the lifeblood of the company, I needed to be completely inaccessible.

I negotiated the deal and dropped out of the picture, even changing my personal phone number to avoid the calls. I made myself untouchable to people who had trusted me and shared their lives with me. It seemed smart at the time. But now that I was on the receiving end of that exact type of treatment, I realized what a mistake it had been.

Surgical approaches to matters of the human heart might be effective in the operating amphitheater, but fail dismally when it comes to relationships. At the time it seemed rational to make a clean cut with major changes. My strategy was to cut, cauterize, and avoid spill-over through months of transition. That isn't much different than trying to dam a river and not expect it to affect what's going on upriver. You can imagine the repercussions of the resulting flooding.

What's inside of you is what flows through you. Hurting people hurt others. Repairing and rebuilding from the damage in these situations that I described took years. The lessons will last a lifetime.

The first lesson is that when you are making decisions that affect other people, communication is critical. Even if the others don't get a vote or a voice in the outcome, they need to be informed. In a family, parents who communicate with their children about the realities influencing choices that affect everyone will have healthier relationship dynamics through life. So it goes for a business culture. Springing major change on people without the benefit of discussion is selfish.

When decisions are handed down in the fashion of a dictatorship, seeds of resentment and rebellion are planted. In the case of a change involving someone leaving, it can cause feelings of abandonment and betrayal.

Courageous communication means talking about the hard stuff. It calls for including others instead of blocking their access to information on things that affect them.

The second lesson learned is this: the law of sowing and reaping plays out, whether you are aware of it or not. When I experienced the painful circumstance of losing a trusted mentor overnight, I could have blamed, pointed fingers, or even considered taking him to court. Instead, I looked within myself to ask, "What could I have done differently to prevent this from happening?" It was only with quiet, time, and introspection, I was able to take responsibility for my part in the outcome.

The third lesson in all of this involves forgiveness. Was I wronged by the mentor that left me hanging? Yes, I think I was. Would it serve any purpose to hold a grudge? Absolutely not.

I can't even number how many little girls I've heard singing the song from the movie *Frozen*, "Let it go, let it go..." I haven't sat through the movie to see the whole message, but if that truth penetrates their young hearts, the movie has value far beyond being a box-office hit. It is said that unforgiveness is like drinking poison and expecting the other person to die.

Forgiving yourself often takes more grace than forgiving others. In either case, begin by making a choice as an act of your will. Don't expect to feel all happy and free just because you make the choice. It takes time for it to work into your emotions. Healing is usually incremental rather than instantaneous.

Rejection isn't fatal—you and I are living proof of that. I think it often takes a will of steel to press through negativity and continue to put yourself out there when you are still reeling from the last rebuff. Overcoming rejection poses two major challenges: the temptation to quit and the temptation to guard your heart to the point it becomes hard and stony.

As your impact and influence expand, rejection and criticism increase as well. Rejection affects us in proportion to the emotional investment we've made in a person or entity. All of us have those times when we've invested heavily and lost big. The saddest thing is to retreat to count your losses and refuse to try again. You and I both have scars no one else can see. These are part of being alive and become part of our life story. Scars don't hurt, but are like badges that entitle you to help others heal like you did. That's called leadership.

Do you still feel a stab of pain when recalling incidents when you felt rejected and abandoned?

Chapter 10
Blind Spots

∾

"The beginning of wisdom is found in doubting; by doubting we come to the question, and by seeking we may come upon the truth."
— Pierre Abelard

Living can be dangerous business. I've been fortunate in the area of auto accidents—I've only been in a few. It doesn't change the damage done to say they weren't my fault. Undoubtedly, all were caused by someone who wasn't paying close enough attention. In one case, I was sideswiped because I was in the person's blind spot. As a result, I drive more defensively than I once did. It's been years since I assumed everyone would stay in their own lane. Dealing with crazy drivers is commonplace, but I happen to be especially thankful for all the times my own mistakes haven't cost me what they might have. Blind spots can be really expensive.

The employee who's stealing.

The spouse who's an alcoholic.

The malignancy that's growing.

Ignorance is not bliss and what you don't know *can* hurt you. In the physical realm, a loss of sight in a part of the visual field is called a scotoma. Every single one of us is afflicted with mental and emotional scotomas—areas where we miss important cues that can cost us. For a number of reasons, we simply don't see things that may be obvious to others. Being the last to be aware of something you should have been the first to know can be disastrous.

One of the first employees I ever hired taught me a memorable lesson about blind spots. I was so thrilled to have help, I was oblivious to the fact that she was rude to my clients and lousy at organizing. In reality, she was more of a liability than an asset. I was clueless for longer than I care to admit. It wasn't until after I let her go that all the stories came out. Suddenly, my clients and peers felt free to tell me details of the many ways she had offended them and handled business inefficiently. These people didn't want to be critical or negative. And I failed to ask the important questions.

A brilliant friend had a trusted employee managing his office who embezzled close to $100,000 before she was caught. It's said that wisdom is learning from the mistakes of others, so I want to know…how did that happen? How do you excise blind spots? How do you know what you don't know? How do you become aware of critical things you might be missing?

Bold leaders develop discernment and discipline to search out the hidden things that could bring down relationships, teams, and ultimately, organizations.

Chief among reasons for blind spots are our own strongly held beliefs. We don't really see things as they are—we see what we want to see. Isaac Asimov describes it by saying, "Your assumptions are your windows on the world. Scrub them off every once in a while, or the light won't come in."

Another phenomenon that causes blind spots is defined as inattentional blindness. We can be so focused on looking for what we have identified as important that we can completely overlook other situations clamoring for attention. Daniel Simons conducted an experiment on this subject that became the title of his book, *The Invisible Gorilla.* A 26-second video clip of one of his experiments went viral on YouTube with almost 11.5 million views, making the subject of inattentional blindness famous. In the test, viewers were instructed to observe two teams passing a basketball and count how many times the white team passed the ball. During the session, a man dressed as a gorilla walks through the middle of the group. The vast majority of people who viewed the clip didn't even notice the gorilla because their attention was deflected to another task. It's disturbing to think about the number of important cues we overlook every single day because we're looking the other way.

Inattentional blindness is actually a timeless version of distraction. Since we live in the most distracted culture of all time, it's more important than ever to tune into what's vital and not allow busyness to steal whatever is valuable to us. Distraction is a primary cause of blind spots, but as if that isn't enough to deal with...there's more.

Emotional blind spots can occur when you have suffered trauma or deep hurt and subsequently blocked deep emotions. There are probably people in your life who seem aloof or uncaring. Often, they're suffering from an emotional shutdown. It's a blind spot for them—they are typically not even aware of it. Some understanding and compassion are called for—though our natural reaction is irritation.

Unfortunately, it is hard to get others to acknowledge what they refuse to see. Alcoholics Anonymous has learned this well—they will offer support for those with a loved one afflicted with alcoholism. But healing cannot occur until the person with the problem seeks help for themselves.

Yet another type of blind spot is what I call the Peter Pan patch. This is worn by people who refuse to grow up in a certain area. Visualize a little child wearing an adult body costume. It's funny to imagine but it's far from humorous to see the destructive nature of a 40-year-old with the reasoning capabilities of a 12-year-old. This is actually a good picture of what has happened when severely dysfunctional relationships in childhood cause people to get stuck emotionally. The physical body matures while the scared, hurt little child cowers inside. Once again, this is most likely a severe blind spot for that individual. Unhealthy relationships and abuse cause deep-seated issues and blind spots that can become black holes if not dealt with.

The conundrum is figuring out how to uncover what you don't know. I've learned some effective strategies along the way to reveal blind spots.

Ask questions. Whether it's your employees or your spouse, it takes courage to ask, "How am I doing? How could I do better? Is there something I do that's creating a problem we haven't discussed?" It's amazing how we can interact with others every single day and fail to ask the hard questions.

Listen more than you talk. Because of my personality type, there's no doubt I have to pay more attention to this one. Stephen Covey, in *7 Habits of Highly Effective People* writes, "Most people don't listen with the intent to understand; they listen with the intent to reply." Ouch. Listening fully is an intentional act. I can remember when my small children would take my chin and turn my face to theirs when they had something important to say. What a powerful reminder to give the person talking the courtesy of our full attention.

Be fully present. One of the symptoms of our ultra-busy lifestyles is the tendency to be mentally disengaged from the moment we are in. I recall a season in my life when I felt I was in an exhausting, never-ending tug of war between the task at hand and the pull of responsibilities awaiting my attention. While at work, I felt guilty that I wasn't taking proper care of my family. Then when family time came, my mind would be on what I had yet to accomplish at work. It's awful. There's no rest when you feel like a rag doll being torn apart at the seams. Just as long-distance truck drivers are more likely to crash if they don't have intervals of rest, so it goes with us. Accept that you can only be one place at a time and give the people you are with your full attention.

Pay attention. This involves more than listening. It means reading the non-verbal cues that others are sending. Psychology 101 teaches that non-verbal communication is about 90% of a message, yet most of us depend on processing words and interpreting verbal structure. Good communication includes paying attention to context, tonality, and non-verbal cues. We simply can't rely on words alone—there's a much bigger picture that should be considered.

Refine your ability to discern. Discernment is the ability to read people and intuitively assess situations. A formal education can train you to read facts and figures, but reading people takes experience and intentionality. Discernment is a companion of wisdom. It's not about mental agility, IQ, or head knowledge. Pay attention to "gut feelings." Cleverness is not wisdom; wisdom is far deeper. You have to choose to refine the skill, and that comes through sensitivity and awareness. One way I do this is by getting quiet and meditating on a person or a situation. It's amazing the revelation you can receive while being still and quieting your mind.

Create a small team of people you trust and can share weighty matters with. This might be a friend, coach, spouse, co-worker, or a select mastermind group. It's priceless to cultivate relationships with those who bring out the best in you and will speak the truth in love to you.

I'm the queen of positive thinking. That means I'm positive I don't know it all and need to constantly get out the magnifying glass to excise blind spots. I've learned the hard way that to willingly blind myself to painful realities that affect me and my team is nothing short of foolish. Armed with awareness, one can make sound decisions and steer clear of hazards.

It's said that the wisest mind always has something new to learn. We have to be aware of our strengths, weaknesses, and blind spots. Human fallibility is not eliminated by power or position. Whether one is driving, debating social issues, family rules, or company policy–blind spots are pervasive and dangerous.

If we are too busy or too lazy to crank our necks and take a hard look at what's going on in the periphery of our vision, it's only a matter of time before we crash.

As we stay open-minded, through the conscious acknowledgement that we don't have all the answers, we will discover truths that elude the arrogant.

What questions have you not dared to ask? Who will you trust to help reveal the blind spot that is a danger area in your life?

Chapter 11
Change

"The pessimist complains about the wind; the optimist expects it to change; the realist adjusts the sails."
— William A. Ward

Most of us are familiar with the five stages of grief and not merely from an intellectual perspective. It was when my dad died that I became personally acquainted with the work of Elisabeth Kübler-Ross and her classic book, *Death and Dying*. I still recall the "aha" moment when I realized our family was experiencing part of the normal process of dealing with unwanted and difficult change. It didn't necessarily make the process easier, but somehow knowing that others had been through this and found their way out of the maze of confusion and loss offered a form of comfort.

Having given much thought to how those five stages apply to the grief we feel when we suffer deep disappointments in our lives, I've looked for the research on dealing with change. It's interesting that most of what is published refers to the kind of change that is personally initiated, like breaking bad habits or battling addiction. Meeting the torpedoes of life, the unexpected challenges over which you have no control, is another matter.

Have you ever found yourself in the midst of a situation you didn't sign up for? You know—the kind that makes you feel like you just fell out of a tree and got the wind knocked out of you. There you are—on your back looking at stars—trying to suck in air, wondering what just happened. The really tough part is that those incidents can be relentless.

There are hundreds of scripts: the great boss you've worked with for seven years suddenly announces she's leaving in three weeks, the job that is eliminated in a structural reorganization, the illness that strikes a family member and turns your world upside down. Each of us has a story to tell about the changes we've dealt with that have shaped who we are. Navigating change certainly makes us stronger, but some days you want to crawl into the cocoon of the familiar and hide there.

As leaders, we are encouraged to step out of our comfort zone. Truth is, if you are actively engaged and intent on growing, you can rest assured you'll find yourself on the edge of a cliff, fearfully looking at the distance to the ground, praying for your life. That's the price of being an eagle. Eagles teach their young to fly with tough love. They remove the padding from the nest until it's prickly and uncomfortable. If that isn't enough to get the young birds to venture from the nest, they are unmercifully pushed out. Fly or perish—those are the choices. And so it goes with us. Fly or perish.

Some lessons are grasped more easily than others. Either way, agility is a leadership quality that is in demand in every sector of our society. Typically, the hardest circumstances refine us the most. Seasons change, relationships break, business models become outdated, jobs end, responsibilities shift. Learning to keep your balance through it all is a key to happiness.

Learning the process for navigating change with grace includes recognizing the five stages. These five stages are: Denial, Anger, Deliberation, Action and Acceptance.

Denial–History tells the tales of many sane, smart leaders who refused to accept facts that threatened their entire careers and organizations. The video distribution giant, Blockbuster, is a vivid example of a company that didn't change with the times. Technology, specifically the internet, has accelerated the pace of change. The graveyard of companies that haven't been willing to adapt quickly to changing times is vast. I've certainly been guilty of digging in my heels in an attempt to defy learning yet another program or updating again.

The denial syndrome is most sharply defined in how people react to disaster. On board the *Titanic*, hundreds of guests danced and demanded first-class service while the ship went down. More recently the same type of behavior was noted during the *Costa Concordia* shipwreck off the coast of Italy.

In the moment following a catastrophe, something happens in our brains that affects the way we think. We behave differently, often irrationally. Consider those who had the terrible misfortune to be in the World Trade Center on the morning of September 11, 2001, who dithered at their desks, calling relatives, turning off computers, and pondering which mementos to rescue from their desks as the inferno raged.

All of these are illustrations of the first response to change–denial. It is one of the greatest obstacles to effective action.

Anger–The second stage of responding to change is one in which emotions reign. Anger can be manifested through accusation, frustration, and blame. Though none of these are productive, it's important to recognize the need to vent emotion. Sometimes the anger directed at oneself is the most dangerous of all. You can beat yourself up to the point you lose your self-confidence. If you don't recognize anger as one of the stages of adapting to change, there's the risk of a downward spiral through regret to despondency. Not a good place to set up camp.

Deliberation–The third stage is the place of decision-making. Weighing options, strategizing, and making a plan–even if it doesn't seem like the best plan–spells progress. Stress causes tunnel-vision, so learning to consider all available choices is a valuable skill. There are *always* choices. The most basic of all is the choice between hope and fear.

Strong leaders are credited with the ability to make quick decisions under pressure. With repeated opportunities to think on our feet, we learn to respond with confidence. Mistakes will be made, but as Will Rogers said, "Even if you're on the right track, you'll get run over if you just sit there."

Action–This stage finds you moving. Overwhelmed people stop. Motivation to get going indicates great progress into the fourth stage of navigating change effectively. A word of caution is due here. Hanging onto the old while moving into the new is not uncommon but highly ineffective. Imagine if you try to keep one foot on the ground and one foot on a train that's preparing to leave the station. You must choose– are you staying or going? If it starts moving while you're undecided, you're going to suffer some serious pain. At this stage, you may not be happy about what's happening, but acceptance is not far off once you're in motion.

Acceptance–The fifth stage positions you in a place of strength. Acceptance opens your mind to new possibilities as you once again find joy in the journey. You are able to perceive and make necessary course adjustments as you go.

All of us undergo a five-stage process when we find ourselves facing change: Denial, Anger, Deliberation, Action, and Acceptance. A key to success and happiness is learning to acknowledge the process, make the best of detours, and turn adversity into advantage.

What area of your life is begging for change, as soon as you come out of denial and face the music?

Chapter 12
No Offense

"Whenever anyone has offended me, I try to raise my soul so high that the offense cannot reach it."
— *Rene Descartes*

When I was a kid in the back of the station wagon on family road trips, I always put my imagination to work as we drove through the towns on the way to our destination. We didn't usually travel on the interstate—my dad favored the scenic route over speed.

As we passed yards strewn with toys, front porches with empty rockers, or a main street with customers moving in and out of the century-old drugstore, my vivid imagination would begin to paint in the details of the lives of those people. I entertained thoughts of what it would be like to go to school in that town, walk the neighborhood, and live in one of those houses. I pictured the personalities and families that built their lives there.

Sometimes, I cringed at the thought of what their lives were like and other times I thought it would be a grand adventure to be in their shoes.

As we journey through life, we meet those people. We work with those people. Sometimes we marry those people. They come from radically different backgrounds than our own. They have different beliefs, attitudes, and experiences—different pains and burdens to carry. And that's just one reason why it's easy for people to offend us.

But here's the deal. When you choose to be offended (and you *can* choose *not* to), you forfeit your ability to influence. When you get offended, you are really passing judgment on the other person. And when you judge people, they feel rejected and they shut down in the relationship. It's especially dangerous when this happens with those we're close to. Sometimes it's the people closest to us who know exactly where to aim to hit our soft spots and inflict injury.

So how do you get through a day without being offended? The key is learning how to respond instead of react. "If you choose to not be offended, then you have taken the first step towards influence." (Jeremy Statton)

I call the art of not being offended "sitting down on the inside." When you sit down on the inside, you liberate yourself by letting go of the need to be right. It's a choice to put down a prideful attitude (EGO with a capital "E") and listen to another person. Even if they're wrong. You may feel justified when you are offended by someone's words or actions. You may feel vindicated when you react. But if you are interested in building enduring relationships, there has to be a better way.

Learning to "sit down on the inside" will set you free. Once you are free, do you always get to stay in that place where you are 100% at peace with yourself and at least 75% at peace with others? In your dreams. The reality is, it takes continual effort.

Here are three principles to guide you that set the standard for "no offence, no foul."

1) Say "I'm sorry" first, even if it's not your fault. Forgive—even if the other person is wrong. It takes a big person to build a bridge and repair a breach. "An offended heart is the breeding ground of deception." (John Bevere)

2) Walking in love is far more valuable than being right.

3) I don't have to defend myself. It's not about me. Every single person has value, even when it's buried under a pile of garbage. Choose to be a treasure hunter for the good that's buried in other people.

It is exhilarating to let go of the need to be right. You cannot change someone else but you *can* choose a new way to respond.

Give freely, and it will come back to you in ways you can't even imagine or measure.

Who are you going to give the gift of forgiveness to today?

Chapter 13
Respect

∞

"Good manners reflect something from inside—an innate sense of consideration for others and respect for self."
— Emily Post

In 35 years of business ownership, I've seen a lot of change. It's hard to even remember a time we didn't rely on technology. I laugh when I think of my first cell phone. It was the size of a shoe with an antenna the size of an umbrella handle. And all you could use it for was phone calls—imagine that! As devices have gotten progressively more sophisticated and supposedly improved our connectedness, the sad reality is they haven't done much for improving the intrinsic value of our communications.

One thing technology hasn't changed is the importance of relationships. Regardless of how many gadgets you own, success revolves around relationships. This applies to success in business, marriage, parenting—everything. The vast changes I've seen pale in comparison with the changes my grandmother witnessed in her lifetime of 103 years. She didn't like cell phones and had no interest whatsoever in computers. But you could glean more wisdom from her than you could ever find on Google. She understood people. Thus she understood respect. And she was a stickler on good manners.

The intersection of these three is where enduring, healthy relationships are built. Let's talk about life at the corner of Respect and Courtesy. Webster's dictionary defines respect as esteem, consideration, and regard. One definition says "to refrain from interfering with."

There's no better illustration of this principle than the nitty-gritty days of raising teenagers. I can't think of a more significant example of the crucial role of respect in relational success. My husband and I, by the grace of God, are the parents of three amazing children who have become responsible adults we admire, respect, and enjoy being with. A principle I applied during their critical transitional years is that to be respected, you have to give respect.

It is a foundational human need to be valued. Though I was keenly aware that I knew best and had more wisdom and experience in my pinky finger than these teenagers had in their heads, I needed to listen to what was important to them. I had to treat them as intelligent, gifted people in order to stay truly engaged with them. A dictatorship only works for the short-term and ultimately results in rebellion. That's the way it is in the workplace as well. Employees who feel disrespected don't stick around.

So how do you demonstrate respect for others in practical ways? Begin by giving people space to make their own decisions. Of course, that means they are going to make mistakes. Micromanaging others causes them to feel manipulated and controlled and communicates a lack of respect.

Demonstrating good manners is another way of respecting others. Clarence Thomas, an Associate Justice of the United States Supreme Court said, "Good manners will open doors that the best education cannot."

Now this is where my grandmother comes back into the story. She was an educator, teaching high school English to generations of students, and a little Southern lady with a big legacy. It is easy for me to imagine her as a contributing writer for *Miss Manners' Guide to Excruciatingly Correct Behavior*. Just to be clear–that's not on her resume. She drilled my mother in etiquette, who subsequently drilled me in the same way I proceeded to drill my children in the finer points of politeness.

Good manners are a practical way of communicating respect regardless of the method: face to face, over the phone, written messages, or online communications. There have always been those who set the gold standard for manners. I'd like to nominate Robert Fulghum, author of *All I Really Need to Know I Learned in Kindergarten*. His list of rules includes:

> "Share everything. Play fair.
> Don't hit people.
> Put things back where you found them.
> Clean up your own mess.
> Don't take things that aren't yours.
> Say you're sorry when you hurt somebody.
> Hold hands and stick together.
> Be aware of wonder."

Just think about the respect and goodwill that could be generated in the world if these simple courtesies became commonplace. Manners cost nothing, but failure to learn and apply them could cost you everything. If everyone obeyed The Golden Rule, *Do unto others as you would have them do unto you*, it would provide a strong start to building a respectful culture.

In our technology-driven culture, there are now apps for manners, though from all appearances, they're not being used much. At times, the Generation called "The Millennials"– those born between 1982 and 2000–have been accused of sacrificing manners and courtesy in lieu of their love for technology. For the record, I think that's an inaccurate and unfair generalization. This is a cultural problem, not a generational one. Along with many Baby Boomers, I've fully embraced technology and consider it a responsibility to translate the intent of good manners into our digital world. Good manners can't be bought, but they can be caught and they can be taught. A combination of both is most effective.

That's why etiquette should be a required course, not an elective, for everyone. From young people creating an immutable footprint in a digital culture to businesses communicating the essence of their brand, there are things you *must* know.

Learning and living out the ABCs of Magnificent Manners is a powerful means of showing others you care. You might consider some of these old-fashioned; however, I maintain good manners never go out of style. The creation of this list was inspired by my popular list of the ABCs of Social Media Manners and became a fun and fascinating family affair when I recruited my 85-year-old mom to help me with it.

ABCs of Magnificent Manners:

Arrive on time. You might argue that in some cultures this is negotiable. In America, it is a show of respect to be on time. Just do it.

Be yourself. Do what you say, say what you mean, be what you seem. And make the effort to be your *best* self.

Criticism is often meant to be constructive but rarely is. If you don't have something nice to say, maybe you're better off not saying anything at all.

Dress appropriately for the venue. If you are in

leadership in a situation, dress at least as nicely as the people in the group. Your clothing is a non-verbal communication tool. Ladies, that has a host of implications for us, but I'll summarize with: modesty is the best policy.

Engage in real conversation with the people you are with. Resist being so addicted to your smart phone that you miss the life that's happening right in front of you.

Filter your words. Be nice. Being authentic doesn't mean saying whatever comes to mind.

Grammar is not the most important thing, but it does say something about you. Anyone who chooses to make the effort can increase their knowledge and become more adept.

Honor others by using their name and making eye contact when speaking to them.

Interrupting others while they are talking is rude. Wait your turn.

Jibe means to agree, as in agree to be civil. You can disagree without being disagreeable.

Keep private conversations private. When on your cell phone in public, recognize when it's time to move to a private space to have a conversation.

Listen carefully. If you receive an emotion-laden message through text, email, digital or written communication, follow up in person or by phone. Digital communication eliminates almost all the nuances of non-verbal communication and can lead to misunderstandings of grand proportion.

Money is a topic to be handled with tact. Generally speaking, it's impolite to ask what someone paid for something. It's rude to discuss salaries and income in a social situation.

Negativity is toxic. Nix the negativity.

Open doors for others, both literally and figuratively.

Courtesy is not a rule limited to age or gender.

Please and *thank you* are still magical words. *May I help you, excuse me,* and *forgive me* round out the top five.

Questions–ask key questions. Ask people how you can help them. Instead of assuming, ask.

Respect others by introducing them with proper titles. And remember to introduce yourself as well.

Silence is golden. Turn off your mobile devices before going into a meeting or appointment. It should go without saying to unplug before a wedding, funeral, or church service. Do whatever it takes to develop this habit–there's a premium on this one!

Tame your temper–it can cost you more than you want to pay. Think before you speak. Pause and respond instead of reacting.

Understanding and patience go a long way. When you see someone blatantly violating protocol, assume they need a mentor more than a critic.

Vulgar is a word in my mother's book defined by indiscretions such as chewing gum while talking, chewing food with your mouth open, or heaven forbid, using a toothpick in public. Currently, the word has implications darker than a mere faux pas, but it is memorable. Educate yourself on the cultural practices of the people you are with and act accordingly to avoid social blunders that make you appear uncouth.

Write handwritten thank-you notes to acknowledge gifts or kind deeds.

X out the cursing. Cussing is guaranteed to offend some people, so leave it out. I was taught that it reveals either laziness or ignorance; people who are too lazy to choose more descriptive vocabulary or those who lacked the educational opportunities to learn resort to cursing.

Yes, ma'am and yes, sir show respect, not just deference to age. Yes is adequate. Never yeah or yep.

Zingers—sarcasm didn't make the manners manual. Hold the sarcastic remarks.

(Credit: Shared authorship with Bettye R. Banks.)

Obviously, this is not a comprehensive list but, as the ABCs, it offers a foundation to build a solid place on the corner of Respect and Courtesy.

Technology will continue to change every time you blink. Manners remain steadfast and unchanging. When you approach manners with the awareness that they are a gateway to valuable connections and meaningful relationships with fascinating people, you will stand out like a beacon and reap untold benefits.

What letter from the list of ABCs is rusty from disuse and begs attention in your life?

Chapter 14
Partnerships

"If you want to go fast, go alone. If you want to go far, go together."
— African Proverb

It began as a daylong excursion to an island paradise set like a jewel in the Gulf Stream off the coast of Florida. Joseph had made the trip countless times to spend a day snorkeling, fishing, and swimming away from the crowded local beaches. He was supremely confident in his knowledge of the waters as well as his boating skills.

This particular day, the boat was loaded with two families, including five children under the age of ten. Enthusiasm ran high until about 90 minutes into the trip, the motor sputtered and died, miles from shore with no land in sight. The mothers on board glanced uneasily at each other while Joseph removed the engine cover, assuring them they would be on their way again in no time. An hour later, drifting in the current with the sun beating down relentlessly, the vessel began to take on water. As the men began to bail and life jackets were retrieved, a somber mood prevailed as the realization hit that there were not enough to go around.

As one of the children on that boat, I developed an early respect for the inherent dangers accompanying the vast beauty of the ocean. That situation held a memorable lesson on the importance of who you travel with.

After experiencing both successful and unsuccessful business partnerships, I know it's critical to team with people you trust. People who have your back and won't just do their best, but will do whatever it takes to make things work out well.

Partnering with the right people takes discernment. The length of the trip and the risks involved are factors that exponentially increase the critical nature of choosing well. The personalities of those you are with, where they are positioned on the team and their commitment to preparation and excellence can mean the difference between reaching your destination or becoming another statistic of a business that sunk. Whether it's a large or small venture, the principles that guide your choices are the same.

When the luxury cruise ship, *Costa Concordia*, capsized just off an island on the western coast of Italy in 2012, it was a routine voyage on a well-traveled route in calm seas. A lapse in judgment by Captain Schettino caused the ship to strike a reef, ripping a 160-foot hole in the ship's port side below the water line. Thirty-two people died, and the property loss exceeded 500 million dollars.

The stormy wreck of major business giants Bear Stearns and Lehman Brothers in 2008 create interesting parallels. Wrong motivations and bad decisions by the CEOs of those companies had terrible repercussions, creating a disastrous wave effect. The beginning of the Great Recession is closely tied to the shipwreck of these two financial giants.

Who is captaining your ship? Your vessel might be a 30-

foot sailboat and bear little resemblance to a massive cruise liner, but the value of the souls aboard can't be measured. Additionally, you would never want to be the cause of economic devastation for anyone, but particularly those you care about.

My husband and I take frequent trips on the nearby Econfina—a clear, cold, spring-fed tributary that is part of the Northwest Florida Water Management area. The winding creek calls for a canoe—probably one of the easiest boats to tip over in. I would not feel safe getting in a canoe with very many people, but I can trust Jim. He sits in the back so he can steer well—a required and critical skill on the northern portion of the river that is filled with fallen trees and obstacles. Jim is also expert at packing our belongings, securing everything in waterproof bags. I am an optimist through and through, but experience has taught me to expect the best while preparing for the worst.

In all of our canoe trips, we've only capsized once. It wasn't a bad decision or a mistake on our part. We were navigating a tight bend in the river, hugging the shore when we startled a large dog on the bank. Growling, he leapt right at me. Of course I reacted by leaning away while Jim lunged to protect me. All that scrambling toppled the canoe. We went into damage control mode while trying to grab our stuff, avoid the agitated dog and get back in the boat. Thankfully, we were in shallow water and the only damage was the bruises I got when I fell over the side. In fact, it was good preparation and being packed well that minimized the problems. That escapade made me appreciate assets in my good choice of a partner; he is good at thinking ahead and planning, he has my back and knows how to make adjustments, deal with setbacks, and move forward. Not all of my business partnerships have fared as well.

This last boating adventure is a parable rather than an account of actual events. Picture a large wooden canoe on a river in Central America–filled with a team of powerful leaders on a crucial mission. Illness incapacitated the team captain. As the current carried the boat toward a large rock formation in the middle of the river, everyone aboard fastened life vests and prepared for impact. They made a tentative plan to regroup after the wreck. Though every last person on board was capable of extraordinary leadership, no one stepped into that role. The canoe splintered as it hit the obstruction, and everyone was thrown into the water. Everyone suffered injuries as they made their way to shore, but there were no casualties. Figuratively, I was in that boat. I was one of the leaders who saw it coming and didn't act fast enough.

There are deep lessons in our failures. Whenever you have a team, someone has to be in charge. That's why a democracy has a President, a company has a CEO, and a team has a captain. A committee that has brilliant ideas will not be effective without a leader to steer the action.

When choosing those you partner with, it is essential that you use discernment and wisdom. And when you get it wrong, you must find the courage to get up, evaluate what you are to learn and carry on.

Here are some things to consider when you are weighing the possibility of a partnership: Test the relationship by getting to know each other in various circumstances. Take a road trip together if possible. There's no better way to learn a lot about a person than to spend time with them through the rigors of travel. You see their ups and downs as well as how they react to situations that don't go as planned. If you are annoyed after a couple of days in their company, you may want to rethink going into business together.

If you can't trust them with your life, don't trust them with your business.

Weigh your skills, talents, and personality characteristics, and look for a good balance. It's not important that you think alike but you do have to be synchronized.

Assess their track record with enduring relationships. Can you expect them to stick around when the going gets tough? You can bet that you will run into challenges so plan for it.

Be certain that you share core values. This is the glue that will stick through thick and thin. Talk about the hard stuff before you commit to journey together. Ask "what if" questions relentlessly.

In the course of owning multiple businesses over the years, I've had strong partnerships that stood the test of time as well as those that dissolved under pressure. The ability to learn the lessons, take another chance, and get back in a boat might be attributed to the story I began with.

Remember Joseph and his overloaded boat drifting in the ocean, sinking slowly with my 7-year-old self on board? It wasn't until years later that I realized how close we came to tragedy that day. We were most fortunate that we were able to stay afloat for hours until another recreational boat spotted us as we wildly waved for help. They managed to tow us to an uninhabited island where we spent the night while they left to report our location and send help. As a kid, I thought it was an exciting adventure. Though my mother vowed to never go anywhere under any circumstances ever again with Joseph, she didn't allow fear to deter her from enjoying a lifetime of adventures on the water. I believe that's called resilience.

The choice of those you travel with—in life and business—plays a huge role in the success of your journey.

Are you partnered with those who have the skill and the will to see you safely to your destination?

Chapter 15
Happiness

"Happy Lady" has been my moniker for decades and I rather like it. If my time on earth ended today and that became my legacy, I'd know it was a life well-lived. Happiness is everything it's cracked up to be–and more.

You can bet I've been criticized for being too happy. Some, who don't know me, think it's phony. I haven't attempted to be less happy to please them. Others think it's a childish and naïve way to deal with life. I prefer the term "childlike." Children are carriers of joy, wonder, and curiosity. For a season, their hope and faith are unspoiled by the harshness of the world. They tend to forgive easily and even forget injustices against them. I won't apologize for holding onto that kind of positive attitude in the face of challenge.

I'll concede that our personality type influences how we express happiness. Regardless of the differences in temperaments, all personality types can live in a state of happiness–it's not the exclusive territory belonging to a few. In fact, you are designed and created for happiness.

If happiness is the goal, let's look at some of the stepping stones to a happy life. First, is the realization that happiness is not a destination but a manner of traveling. By the time we are teenagers, most of us are looking at life backwards. We buy into the mind-set that says, "When I get this, do that, or become this...*then* I'll be happy." In reality, when we become happy, *then* we're more likely to be successful at whatever we are in pursuit of: the right job, satisfying relationships, more income, or whatever it might be.

Perspective is everything. Dale Carnegie said, "It isn't what you have, or who you are, or where you are, or what you are doing that makes you happy or unhappy. It's what you think about." The world bombards us with negative messages at an overwhelming pace. It takes a conscious effort to disengage from the negativity and focus on the good. We become what we think about.

Our thoughts direct our lives in the same way that when driving, you steer toward what you're looking at. Race car drivers will tell you that focus is critical not only to winning but to survival. Keep your eyes on where you want to go. Not on where you've been or on the ditch of negativity.

Forgiveness is like a daily bath–you'll develop an odor if you skip too many. I've found the proverb "Don't let the sun go down on your anger" and the age-old marriage advice "Never go to bed angry" almost impossible to heed. However, I look at every day as a fresh slate and a chance to start over. Early morning is my time to accept the apologies I never got and enjoy the freedom of forgiveness. It makes me smile to recall a friend's experience with learning to hear the voice of God. He decided to ask a direct, practical question and inquired of God, "Why did you create day and night?" He recounts God's response, "Every 24 hours, you need a chance to start over." I need that chance and I'm guessing you do, too. Oh, and while you're at it, develop the practice of forgiving yourself, too. It will set you free and will boost your happiness more than any other thing I know.

Music is another powerful tool for taking you into the land of happiness. Music is my first language—English is a second language in my world. I've known since I was very young that music is an important part of my DNA. It is for you as well—even if you haven't been conscious of that fact. Did you know that your DNA is actually a musical coding that vibrates at a unique frequency? Consider the Latin root of the word "person." "Per" means passes through. "Sona" is sound. "Person" literally translates as one whom sound passes through. This explains why music has such a deep effect on our moods, emotions, and even our ability to learn. You can use this knowledge as part of your strategy to cultivate happiness. Tune into your responses to different types of music and become intentional about what you listen to.

Edit the words that come out of your mouth. Words can be a weapon that injures or a balm that heals; they can build or they can tear down; they ignite passion or smother hope; they instigate sadness or create happiness. Having already talked about the power of thoughts, it might seem redundant to emphasize the weight of words. If thoughts are fuel, speaking them is the ignition switch that sets things into action. Scientific research on how speech influences brain activity and resonates in the environment is nothing short of astonishing. Watch your mouth.

Smile more. Smiling is the highest positive emotional gesture in your repertoire. Using the muscles that initiate a smile will put you in a happier mood, says Dr. Michael Lewis, psychologist at Cardiff University. In a study published in

Psychological Science, the benefits of smiling in stress reduction were proven, measuring a smile's effect on heart rate and respiration, among other things. It's easy for me to get carried away citing the science of happiness because it is only in the last two decades that three separate disciplines—neuroscience, economics and psychology—have joined philosophers and poets in studying what makes people happy.

Life-long learning is more than a noble aspiration—it is another contributor to happiness. Nobel prize-winning author Linus Pauling said, "Satisfaction of one's curiosity is one of the greatest sources of happiness in life."

Gratitude is an attitude that contributes significantly to contentment and happiness. Some people think aging tends to make people grouchy and difficult. I beg to differ. In reality, the habit of discontentment can dictate the lives of anyone of any age who allows it. On the other hand, there's fascinating research in the field of positive psychology that indicates you can increase your happiness level by 25% by focusing on what you are thankful for. One particular study by Emmons and McCullough on "Counting Blessings vs. Burdens: An Experimental Investigation of Gratitude and Subjective Well-Being in Daily Life," indicates that spending a few hours writing a gratitude journal over a period of three weeks can create an effect that lasts at least six months.

Lighten up. Don't take yourself too seriously. Many years ago, I heard a preacher say, "If you take God seriously, you are relieved of the burden of taking anything else too seriously." I decided those were words to live by and developed a perspective that releases me from the responsibility of thinking I'm in charge of every day.

Stop comparing yourself to others. Comparison is the thief of joy. The impact of social media on our ability to form snapshots of the lives of others has expanded our tendency to compare. There is no purpose served in comparing, not to mention that we are usually basing our thoughts on inaccurate and incomplete information. If comparing is how you are evaluating your worth, happiness will always be elusive.

Dream. Set goals. Anticipation of good things that we are looking forward to is a proven way to boost mood and create a feeling of happiness. Our brain has the unique ability to cause the production of endorphins (the feel-good hormone) when we are simply imagining doing something we really enjoy.

If you're waiting for something external to change to become a happier person, you're missing out. Happiness is your destiny, but you have to want to go there and choose the path that leads you to it. No one holds the key to your happiness—it's in your hands. The golden door is before you...

What simple step will you implement today to elevate your happiness quotient?

Chapter 16
Legacy

"I don't want to have lived in vain...I want to be useful or bring enjoyment to all people, even those I've never met. I want to go on living even after my death."
– Anne Frank

Decades ago, I developed an embarrassing habit that persists to this day. I read obituaries regularly. I've often wondered about the motivation behind what seems like a morbid routine. In my defense, I only read the local ones–beginning by skimming for familiar names. It seems important to me to know who has left this world for eternity. I rationalize this is a daily reminder to make every day count. After all, I want to dream like I'll live forever and live like I might die today–appreciating that life is a gift and time is fleeting.

I've even taken this interest so far as to write my own obituary. I was actually participating in an exercise in a goals workshop, so it wasn't my idea. And while I haven't implemented this activity in workshops I conduct, it's actually quite effective for stimulating thinking about how you want to be remembered. "Begin with the end in mind" is good advice for almost any endeavor.

Legacy. We all leave one. The lens of legacy calls us to venture past the mundane into the masterful. It rouses us from lethargy by stirring our responsibility to make a difference. It appeals to us to use our learning as the springboard to mentor others. It enables us to be less concerned with the impression we make and more concerned with the lasting impact we'll have.

Oliver Wendell Holmes wrote, "Many people die with their music still in them. Why is this so? Too often it is because they are always getting ready to live. Before they know it, time runs out." That poignant thought has always resonated deeply with me, perhaps because I understand every human being quite literally carries a life song. Mr. Holmes waxed poetic about a scientific fact that wasn't even yet discovered in his generation.

The lens of legacy causes us to see farther than the boundaries of the present and understand our responsibility to the generations to come. It invites us to appreciate the inheritance we've received from those who have plowed and planted before us. It challenges us to perpetuate the pioneering spirit with clear vision and bold action.

"Thinking generationally is the pattern and blueprint for wealth, prosperity, and blessing," states John Muratori, strategic planner and organizational management consultant. He goes on to say, "Generational wealth consists of more than money, but encompasses the philosophies, moral values, and leadership of a culture. It is vital that positive components be passed to ensuing generations."

Recently, I was talking with a cousin who has spent considerable time tracing our family genealogy. He has traveled, etched tombstones, spent hours poring over archives, and done an amazing job of unearthing details. All to document a very colorful family tree, which incidentally, I discovered qualifies me for membership in the DAR (Daughters of the American Revolution). What a legacy. My cousin has an uproariously funny storytelling ability, so he has managed to interest the whole family in our history. I've been reflecting on the value of that gift.

There's power in your story. Yes, yours. Everybody has a story, and nobody can tell your story like you can. Stories are a powerful way of communicating. In this age of information overload, stories have retained their ability to captivate, convince, and inspire. They touch the heart and can engage the listener in a way they will remember.

You might question what's so special about your story. It might be fraught with pain and failure.

There's no such thing as wasted pain if you use the lessons in a redemptive way that helps others overcome the difficulties you've faced.

Your story is as near as your breath. It's part of your legacy. The ancient tradition of storytelling is not a lost art, but a very current way to be heard amidst the clamor. Shannon Alder writes, "Carve your name on hearts, not tombstones. A legacy is etched into the minds of others and the stories they share about you."

The staggering volume of information available by Googling a topic doesn't trump the human connection that storytelling allows. Journaling and blogging are modern versions of storytelling. As important as oral traditions of storytelling have been in anthropology, there are inherent shortcomings. Important truths can be lost in translation and are only one generation shy of being lost forever. Have you ever considered that your blog or journal is making history?

Here's the truth: your story makes a difference. Tell it. Speak it, write it, sing it, paint it. However you can express it—

do it! You might think no one hears you. But your life matters, and your story needs to be told. Whether you're leading a 10-pound terrier or an organization of 100, you have influence.

Leaving a legacy of success can be defined in any number of ways. It's deeply personal. In the past 30 years, I've never found a definition that speaks to me the way Ralph Waldo Emerson's words do:

> To laugh often and much;
> to win the respect of intelligent people and the affection of children;
> to earn the appreciation of old and new friends;
> to appreciate beauty; to find the best in others;
> to leave the world a bit better,
> whether by a healthy child,
> a garden patch,
> or a redeemed social condition;
> to know that even one life has breathed easier because you have lived–
> this is to have succeeded.

Have you learned to articulate your story in a way that speaks to people you can influence?

Chapter 17
The View from the Top

∂

Have you ever set out to do something that took longer than you expected and was harder than you ever imagined? It seems like most worthwhile projects are like that.

In the midst of writing this book, my husband and I spent the better part of a week in the Great Smoky Mountains. A change of pace and stunningly beautiful scenery are always excellent for refreshing one's perspective.

My husband has an extraordinarily adventurous spirit, so every trip with him is an incubator for stories that will be retold and laughed about for years. This particular trip, the story developed on the trail to Rainbow Falls. The planned hike was rated in the guidebook as a moderate level trek. Jim is compelled to push the limits and could have handled an advanced level, but he wanted this day to be an easier one since we were going with friends that weren't accustomed to hiking. (I appreciated the mercy as well!)

The six-mile hike would have been no hardship except

the guidebook left out one not-so-minor detail: the trail led straight up a mountain. I set out with exuberance, high energy and a sense of exhilaration. Three hours later, after a steady climb over rough terrain, I came to a spot where I was staring at the picture I had always imagined would become the cover of this book. It was clear in my head before I began writing, but it stunned me to be looking at the mountain stream, crossable on uneven stones scattered across the riverbed.

As I contemplated the scene before me, I experienced a rush of emotion as I realized I was exhausted and uncertain I could make it safely across. There were others behind me, waiting for me to step out on the rocks. It was only possible to go single file, and I was in the lead. Dismay washed over me as I recognized my weakness and questioned my ability.

Everything within me screamed to me to sit down and rest. Maybe I could just wait by the side of the stream while the others went on without me–I could rejoin them on their way back. But the moment spoke to me of the important things I have been writing of: leadership, achievement, purpose, resolve, focus, and excellence. It wasn't an option to quit, as much as I wanted to. So I called for help. We can be so stubborn about that, can't we? Success is no less satisfying when you've had help to get there. I daresay it's even *more* gratifying to be able to acknowledge the people who help you achieve more than you ever could on your own. My husband, who has been my hero countless times over the years, came to my aid, and I made it across.

You don't climb mountains and ford rivers without a team. You don't climb mountains without being prepared. You don't traverse rivers without taking care of your health. You don't make it to the top without weighing the risk and reward. And you never just happen to find yourself on the summit–you arrive there intentionally. You can absolutely know that the most difficult paths lead to the most spectacular views.

In the pages of this book, I have offered my lessons on success, learned both in the crucible of the wilderness and in the process of building the people who build businesses.

I'll put a rainbow over the content with things I meditated on as I climbed.

Do your research before you set out. Get a map and a vision of the land you'll be traversing. Learn from those who have traveled where you are going. I have been known for my "Ready, Fire, Aim" approach, but there are times that can be deadly. Carry a compass, just in case you get off the trail and the map doesn't serve because you've lost your way. In business, your vision is your map and your core values are your compass. Couple those tools with research and a teachable spirit and you're on your way.

Be alert. Your competitors might eat your lunch but the predators will take you down if you don't pay attention. We were cautioned by a forest ranger while hiking that there were bears in the area. He advised that if we encountered one to make yourself look big and don't run—that would trigger the bear's predator instinct. That's something to ponder...how do you make yourself look bigger than you are? We joked about getting on one another's shoulders—happy we didn't have to test that ability. Standing firm in the face of opposition and not allowing intimidation to put you in flight mode is a skill we can all use daily.

Be prepared—equip yourself with the right tools. I put off the purchase of hiking boots for years, convinced I didn't hike enough to make it worth the investment. Remember that severe sprain on a hike in Alaska I told you about? I was in running shoes—fine for paved roads but not good for rocky ground. I realized it would be smart to get the proper footwear. What a difference! I also discovered the value of good hiker's poles. They increase balance and stability—how important is that? In today's business environment, you need every advantage you can get. Find out what the essential, non-negotiable tools are in your field and find a way to have them. It doesn't make sense to handicap yourself before you've even started.

Pace Yourself. Speed is not your friend on difficult terrain. At the onset of our hike, I watched as a teenager took off running on the rocky trail to catch up with his companions, tripping and falling hard on rocks–twisting his ankle. A dangerous move at an elevation where help is far away. The fast pace of the world around us can deceive us into thinking we have to run to keep up. Costly mistakes can be avoided with deliberation and intentionality. Taking time to pause and rehydrate is another tip that will allow you to sustain your energy.

Make a plan but don't fall in love with the plan. When we began our trek to Rainbow Falls, based on the mileage in the guidebook, we calculated a three-hour hike. We got a little concerned when it took us three hours to reach the summit. We talked with a couple of other hikers who also discovered this particular trail to be more than they bargained for in an afternoon hike. As we were halfway down the mountain, we cautioned a couple of teams on their way up that they might want to consider sunset time and the length of the hike. One team heeded our words and decided to return the next day. Another pair flipped off our caution. I sincerely hope they weren't trying to negotiate the rocky trail after dark with no flashlight. Sometimes we get our mind so set on something, we disregard common sense. It's a good thing to have resolve, but sometimes it's necessary to adjust our plans.

Select your team with care. It's been said that the pace of the leader is the pace of the pack. That is not true in the case of an arduous climb. The leader might be fast but you can't afford to leave anyone behind. Therefore, everyone on the team has to be fit and able to carry their own weight. Another consideration is personality and attitude of the people you go with. I think it's a lot more fun to travel with cheerful people who can keep a good attitude. Whining is tiresome.

Enjoy the journey. You can be so focused on the goal that you forget to look up and take pleasure in the process. The uneven ground on our most recent hike demanded that I pay attention to where my feet were landing, so I paused often to feel the breeze, smell the piney fragrance of the woods, and marvel at the autumn leaves. It's said that happiness is not a destination; it's a manner of traveling.

One last thought...take time to celebrate your success. I don't know that I've ever enjoyed a meal more than the one we ate after that hike. It was simple, filling, and a memorable way to congratulate ourselves on completing an unforgettable adventure.

Victory is sweet—savor it.

38639836R00059

Made in the USA
Charleston, SC
11 February 2015